Food for Life

RAINFORESTS

KATE RIGGS

Published by Creative Education
P.O. Box 227, Mankato, Minnesota 56002
Creative Education is an imprint of The Creative Company
www.thecreativecompany.us

Design and production by Liddy Walseth
Art direction by Rita Marshall
Printed in the United States of America

Photographs by Corbis (Markus Botzek/zefa, Tom Brakefield, Frans Lanting,
Gerd Ludwig, Kevin Schafer), Getty Images (Gerry Ellis, Tim Flach, Michael
& Patricia Fogden, David Hiser, Pete Oxford, Walter Pfisterer, Art Wolfe,
Norbert Wu), iStockphoto (Ewen Cameron)

Library of Congress Cataloging-in-Publication Data
Riggs, Kate.
Rainforests / by Kate Riggs.
p. cm. — (Food for life)
Includes index.
Summary: A fundamental look at a common food chain in the rainforest,
starting with the cacao tree, ending with the powerful jaguar, and
introducing various animals in between.
ISBN 978-1-58341-829-1
1. Rainforest ecology—Juvenile literature. 2. Food chains (Ecology)—
Juvenile literature.
I. Title. II. Series.

QH541.5.R27R54 2010
577.34'16—dc22 2009004782

First Edition
2 4 6 8 9 7 5 3 1

Food for Life

RAINFORESTS

KATE RIGGS

A food chain shows what living things in an area eat. Plants are the first link on a food chain. Animals that eat plants or other animals make up the rest of the links.

A PIRANHA IS A DEADLY
TOOTHED FISH WILL EAT

PREDATOR. THE SHARP-
ANY ANIMAL IN ITS WATERS.

THE QUETZAL (kayt-SAHL) IS A COLORFUL RAINFOREST BIRD. IT EATS FRUITS LIKE AVOCADOS (ah-voh-KAH-dohs).

A rainforest is a hot and wet place. It has tall trees and bright flowers. Rainforests are found in the hottest parts of the world. Most rainforests are near the _equator_ (ee-KWAY-ter).

The **cacao** (kah-KAH-oh) tree
grows in the shady rainforest.
People take the tree's seeds to
make chocolate. Many animals
also eat the tree's fruit. The
fruit is called a cacao pod.

Leafcutter ants eat cacao leaves.
They work together to carry
the leaves back to their nest.
Millions of ants live together
in one underground nest.

GORILLAS ARE BIG, PLANT-
IN RAINFORESTS ON THE

EATING ANIMALS. THEY LIVE _CONTINENT_ OF AFRICA.

The silky anteater is named for its favorite _prey_. It likes to eat ants. The anteater has a tail that is almost as long as its body. Its long tongue can reach into ants' underground nests.

Boa constrictors (con-STRIK-ters) are snakes that move through the rainforest looking for animals to eat. When a boa finds an anteater, it wraps its body around the anteater. It squeezes the animal to death.

A jaguar uses its sharp teeth and claws to catch boas. The big cat is a good hunter. It sneaks up on the boa. Then it jumps on the snake and bites its head.

ONLY A FEW ANIMALS CAN

THE FROG IS DEADLY

EAT THE POISON DART FROG.
TO ALL OTHER ANIMALS.

All of these living things make up a food chain. The cacao tree grows in the rainforest. The leafcutter ant eats the cacao leaves. The silky anteater eats the ant. The boa constrictor eats the anteater. And the jaguar eats the boa.

KING VULTURES ARE
RAINFOREST SCAVENGERS.
THEY EAT THE LEFTOVERS
OF DEAD ANIMALS.

Some day, the jaguar will die. Its body will break down into _nutrients_ (NOO-tree-ents). These nutrients will go into the ground and help plants such as the cacao tree grow. Then the rainforest food chain will start all over again.

READ MORE ABOUT IT

Kalman, Bobbie, and Molly Aloian. *Rainforest Food Chains*. New York: Crabtree Publishing Company, 2006.

Snedden, Robert. *Who Eats Who in the Rainforest?* North Mankato, Minn.: Smart Apple Media, 2007.

GLOSSARY

continent—one of Earth's seven big pieces of land

equator—an area around the middle of Earth

nutrients—things in soil and food that help plants and animals grow strong and healthy

predator—an animal that kills and eats other animals

prey—an animal that is eaten by another animal

INDEX